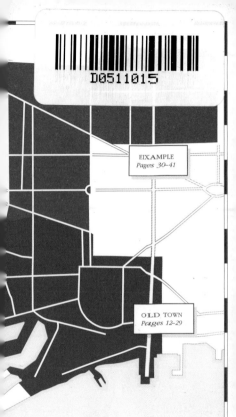

0 metres   750
0 yards   750

EYEWITNESS TRAVEL

BARCELONA

POCKET GUIDE

LONDON, NEW YORK,
MELBOURNE, MUNICH AND DELHI
www.dk.com

PROJECT DIRECTORS Nicholas Bevan, Derek Hall

EDITORS Derek Hall, Sue Juby, Alexander Stillwell

DESIGNER Anita Ruddell

INDEXER Michael Dent

PICTURE RESEARCHER Mirco De Cet

CARTOGRAPHY John Plumer

Conceived and produced by Redback Publishing, 25 Longhope
Drive, Farnham, Surrey, GU10 4SN

Reproduced by Colourscan (Singapore)

Printed and bound in China by Leo Paper Products Ltd

First published in Great Britain in 2006
by Dorling Kindersley Limited
80 Strand, London WC2R 0RL

ISBN-13: 978-1-40531-357-5

ISBN-10: 1-40531-357-9

**The information in this
DK Eyewitness Travel Guide is checked regularly.**
Every effort has been made to ensure that this book is as up-to-date as
possible at the time of going to press. Some details, however, such as
telephone numbers, opening hours, prices, gallery hanging
arrangements and travel information, are liable to change. The
publishers cannot accept responsibility for any consequences arising
from the use of this book, nor for any material on third-party websites,
and cannot guarantee that any website address in this book will be a
suitable source of travel information. We value the views and
suggestions of our readers highly. Please write to:
Publisher, DK Eyewitness Travel Guides,
Dorling Kindersley, 80 Strand, London WC2R 0RL.

Stallholder at a Christmas market in front of the cathedral, Barcelona

CONTENTS

*The new swing Bridge in barcelona's Old Town,
as seen from the water*

Central Barcelona

Barcelona is the capital of Catalonia and one of the Mediterranean's busiest ports. The three main sightseeing areas are Montjuïc, a hilly area of monumental buildings almost enclosing the city; the Old Town, with its Gothic heart and narrow streets; and Eixample, with its stunning Modernista architecture.

Montjuïc Castle
This massive fortification dating from the 17th century offers panoramic views of the city and port (see pp46–7).

Old Town
This area includes all the oldest districts of Barcelona and its port, the 18th-century fishing "village" of Barceloneta and the new waterside developments. This new swing bridge is in the Old Port (see p26).

TRAVESSERA DE GRACIA

CARRER DE ST ANTONI MARIA CLARET

IXAMPLE

CARRER DE CORSEGA

AVINGUDA DIAGONAL

PASSEIG DE SANT JOAN

AVINGUDA DE GAUDI

CARRER DE XIFRE

Sagrada Família

CARRER DE VALENCIA

CARRER D'ARAGO

asa Battló

DEL

VIA DE LES CORTS CATALANES

BRUC

A DE
NYA

VIA LAIETANA

ST PERE MES BAIX

PLAÇA
D'ANTONI
MAURA

C DE LA PRINCESA

**Museu
Picasso**

PLAÇA
M D'ANTONI
LOPEZ

PASSEIG DE PICASSO

PARC DE LA
CIUTADELLA

CARRER DE JOAN MIRO

PARC
ZOOLOGIC

PASSEIG JOAN DE BORBO

PARC DE LA
BARCELONETA

PASSEIG

MARITIM

KEY

▣	Major sight
Ⓜ	Metro station
🚊	Train station
🚏	Bus stop
⛴	Boat boarding point
🚠	Cable car
🚡	Funicular

Eixample

*This area covers the most
interesting part of the city's
19th-century expansion. Walks
along its streets will reveal
countless details of the Modernista style, such as this ornate
doorway of Casa Comalat in
Avinguda Diagonal.*

Barcelona's Highlights

This glittering jewel in the Mediterranean has a wealth of fascinating places to explore – from the buoyant, revamped port area to the medieval streets of the Barri Gòtic and the beautiful *Modernista* buildings of the Eixample.

Museums and Galleries

Palau Nacional, home of the Museu Nacional d'Art de Catalunya

Museu Nacional d'Art de Catalunya

Catalonia's rich Romanesque heritage is on display at this impressive museum, housed in the 1929 Palau Nacional (*see p45*).

Fundació Joan Miró

The airy galleries of this museum are a fitting setting for 20th-century artist Joan Miró's bold, abstract works (*see p44*).

Museu Picasso

Witness the budding – and meteoric rise – of Picasso's artistic genius at this unique museum (*see p24*).

Museu del FC Barcelona

This shrine to the city's football club has trophies, posters and other memorabilia celebrating the club's 100-year history (*see p50*).

Museu d'Història de la Ciutat

Explore the medieval Palau Reial and wander among the remains of Barcelona's Roman walls and waterways at the city's history museum (*see p14*).

Museu Marítim and Drassanes

Barcelona's seafaring past, from the Middle Ages to the 19th century, is showcased in the 13th-century royal shipyards (*see p28*).

Squares

Plaça Reial

The arcaded Plaça Reial, in the heart of the Barri Gòtic, is unique in its mix of old-world charm, gritty urbanization and Neo-Classical flair (*see p19*).

Plaça Reial, Barri Gòtic

Plaça del Rei

One of the city's best preserved medieval squares, the Barri Gòtic Plaça del Rei is ringed by grand buildings, including the 14th-century Palau Reial (*see p14*).

Plaça d'Espanya
The fountain in the middle of this road junction is by Josep Maria Jujol, a follower of Gaudí. Other sculptures and fine buildings abound (see p46).

Plaça de la Boqueria
In the heart of the historic La Rambla, this square has a mosaic pavement by Miró and an Art Deco dragon designed for a former umbrella shop (see p19).

Gaudí

Casa Batlló
Casa Batlló, an allegory of the legend of Sant Jordi, has a roof in the form of a dragon's back and balconies representing the skulls of its victims (see pp32–3).

Palau Güell
This palace is a fine example of Gaudí's experiments with structure. Also remarkable is the use of unusual materials, such as ebony and rare South American woods (see p22–3).

Casa Milà
This amazing apartment block, with its curving façade and bizarre rooftop, has all the Gaudí architectural trademarks (see p40).

Casa Milà rooftop sculpture park

Sagrada Família
Dizzying spires and intricate symbolic sculptures adorn Gaudí's unfinished masterpiece (see pp36–9).

Churches and Cathedrals

Barcelona Cathedral

Barcelona Cathedral
Dominating the heart of the Old Town, Barcelona's magnificent Gothic cathedral boasts an eye-catching façade and a peaceful cloister (see pp16–17).

Basílica de Santa Maria del Mar
This beautiful building, the city's favourite church with superb acoustics for concerts, is the only example of a church entirely in the Catalan Gothic style (see p24).

Monestir de Santa Maria de Pedralbes
This lovely monastery has important art treasures on show and retains the air of an enclosed community (see p51).

Capella de Sant Jordi
Inside the Palau de la Generalitat is a fine 15th-century chapel dedicated to Catalonia's patron saint (see p15).

The Flavours of Catalonia

Food is central to the Catalan soul, and the culinary scene in Catalonia is now one of the most exciting in Europe. The old ways also survive in small, family-run restaurants, authentic, sawdust-strewn tapas bars, and particularly in the superb local markets.

Visit any of Barcelona's excellent markets to see stalls heaped with glistening Mediterranean fish, superb-quality meat and game from the mountains and a quite dazzling array of fruit and vegetables from the plains. Catalan cuisine, even when experimental, is essentially simple, and relies on the quality and range of local produce.

Meat and Game

Catalan cured meats are famous throughout Spain, particularly the pungent cured sausage *fuet*. Pork finds its way on to almost every menu, with *peus de porc* (pigs' trotters) an old-fashioned favourite. Its mountain cousin, wild boar (*porc sanglar*) is popular in late autumn, along with game, especially partridge (*perdiu*). Rabbit (*conill*) and snails (*cargols*), come into their own in hearty winter dishes.

Fish

Barcelona excels at seafood. Tapas bars commonly serve mouthwatering sardines, and rosy prawns grilled or tossed in garlic. Fish is often served grilled (*a la brasa*), or perhaps with a simple sauce. It's especially good cooked paella-style in *fideuà*, or in a stew such as *suquet de peix*. But humble dried, salted cod (*bacallà*), still reigns supreme in Catalan cuisine, and is at its most delicious when baked with tomatoes, garlic and wine (*a la llauna*).

Xoriço picant · Fuet · Llonganissa · Xoriço · Xoriço curat · Pernil salat

Selection of Catalan cured meats, known as embutits

Locally caught sardines being grilled over charcoal

Fruit and Vegetables

Spring is heralded by *calçots*, a cross between leeks and onions, tiny broad (fava) beans and asparagus spears. In summer, market stalls blaze with the colours of cherries, strawberries, figs, peaches and melons, gleaming aubergines (eggplants), courgettes (zucchini), tomatoes and artichokes. In autumn, Catalans seek out wild mushrooms (*bolets*), and classic Catalan bean dishes appear on menus as winter approaches.

Local Dishes and Specialities

A quartet of sauces underpins most Catalan cuisine. King of them all is *sofregit*, a reduction of caramelized onions, fresh tomatoes and

Conill amb cargols is a stew of rabbit and snails with tomatoes, spices and a splash of wine

BEST FOOD SHOPPING

La Boquería (see p19).

Xocoa Carrer d'en Bot. *Excellent chocolate in slick designer packaging (see p29).*

Casa del Bacalao Carrer Comtal. *Traditional temple to bacallà.*

La Pineda Carrer del Pi. *Delightful old grocer's, specializing in hams.*

Tot Formatge Passeig del Born. *Superb cheeses from Catalonia, Spain and elsewhere.*

Botifarrería de Santa María Carrer Santa María. *Cured meats of all kinds.*

Origens 99.9% Carrer Vidreria. *Catalan products, organic where possible, including cheeses, hams, oils and conserves.*

Pa amb tomàquet

herbs. *Samfaina* also has roast aubergines, courgettes and peppers. *Picada* is spicier, and normally has breadcrumbs, garlic, almonds, saffron and pine nuts. *Allí oli* is a garlicky, mayonnaise-like (but eggless) sauce, usually served with grilled meat and vegetables. But the classic Catalan dish is *pa amb tomàquet* – crusty bread rubbed with fresh tomatoes and garlic, then drizzled with olive oil.

A Glossary of Typical Dishes

Catalan cuisine at its best is known
as *cuina de mercat* (market cuisine).
Barcelona's La Boqueria market
excels at such produce (*see pp18–19*).

Tapes (Tapas – Snacks)

Anxoves: anchovies.
Escopinyes: cockles.
Bunyols de bacallà: salt cod
fritters.
Calamars a la romana: fried
squid.
Pa amb tomàquet: bread with
tomato, garlic and olive oil.
Panadons d'espinacs:
spinach pies.
Patatas bravas: potato in
spicy tomato sauce.
Pernil: seasoned pork.
Pescaditos: small fried fish.
Popets: baby octopus.
Truita de patates: potato and
onion omelette.

Entrants (Starters)

Amanida catalana: mixed
salad.
Cargols a la llauna: snails in
sauce.
Empedrat: salt cod and bean
salad.
Escalivada: char-grilled or
roasted aubergines and peppers in olive oil.
Espinacs a la catalana:
spinach with pine nuts, raisins
and ham; sometimes with
chard (bledes).

Esqueixada: *Olives*
salt cod salad.
Faves a la catalana: broad
bean stew.
Garotes: raw sea urchins.
Musclos: mussels.
**Ous remenats amb
camasecs**: scrambled eggs
and mushrooms.

Sopes (Soups)

Escudella i carn d'olla: the
liquid from the traditional hot-
pot; the meat and vegetables
are served as a main course.
Gaspatxo: clear, cold soup
with added raw vegetables.
Sopa de farigola: thyme
soup.
Sopa de bolets: mushroom
soup.

Peix i Mariscos (Fish and Shellfish)

Allipebre d'anguiles: eel
stew.
Anfós al forn: baked stuffed
grouper.
Calamars farcits: squid
stuffed with pork, tomatoes
and onions.
Cassola de peix: fish casserole.
Congre amb pèsols: conger
eel with peas.
Escamarlans bullits: boiled
Dublin Bay prawns
Gambes a la planxa: griddled
prawns.
Graellada de peix: seafood
grill.
Llagosta a la brasa: lobster
cooked over open flames.
Llagostins amb maionesa:
king prawns and mayonnaise.
Llobarro al forn a rodanxes:
baked, sliced sea bass.

*Pa amb tomàquet with ham and
olives makes a delicious tapas dish*

Molls a la brasa: red mullet cooked over open flames.
Orada a la sal: gilthead bream in salt, which is removed on serving.
Paella valenciana: paella with chicken and seafood.
Rap a l'all cremat: angler fish with crisped garlic.
Romesco de peix: seafood with romesco sauce.
Sarsuela: fish, shellfish and spices.
Suquet de peix: fish stew.

Carn (Meat)

Ànec amb naps: duck with turnips.
Boles de picolat: meatballs in tomato sauce.
Botifarra amb mongetes: sausage and beans.
Bou a l'adoba: beef casserole.
Costelles a la brasa amb allioli: flame-roast lamb cutlets.
Cuixa de xai al forn: roast lamb.
Estofat de bou: beef stew.
Estofat de quaresma: Lenten vegetable stew.
Freginat: calf's liver with onions.
Llom de porc: pork chops.
Niu: huge fish and meat stew.
Peus de porc a la llauna: pig's trotters in a spicy sauce.
Pollastre amb samfaina: chicken with samfaina.
Pota i tripa: lamb's trotters and tripe.
Tripa a la catalana: tripe in sofregit and wine with almond and pine nuts.
Xai amb pèsols: lamb with peas.

Produce at La Boqueria, the huge food market on La Rambla

Caça (Game)

Becada amb coc: woodcock in a bread roll.
Civet de llebre: jugged hare.
Conill a la brasa amb allioli: rabbit with garlic mayonnaise.
Conill amb cargols: rabbit with snails.
Conill amb xocolata: rabbit with liver, almonds, fried bread, chocolate and old wine.
Estofat de porc senglar amb bolets: wild boar and mushroom casserole.
Guatlles amb salsa de magrana: quail in pomegranate sauce.
Perdius amb farcellets de col: partridge with cabbage.

Verdures (Vegetables)

Albergínies: aubergines.
Bledes: chard.
Bolets: mushrooms.
Calçots: roasted green onions in a spicy tomato sauce.
Carbassó arrebossat: battered courgettes (zucchini).
Carxofes: artichokes.
Julivert: parsley.
Mongetes tendres i patates: French beans and potatoes.
Pastanagues: carrots.
Pebrots: red peppers.

Postres (Desserts)

Crema catalana: egg custard.
Figues amb aniset: figs in anise.
Flam: crème caramel.
Formatge: cheese.
Gelat: ice cream.
Meli Mató: goat's cheese/honey.
Menjar blanc: almond blancmange.
Peres amb vi negre: pears in wine.

0 metres 500

0 yards 500

◀ Els Quatre
Gats café in
Barcelona's
Barri Gòtic
area

OLD TOWN

Traversed by the famous avenue, La Rambla, this is one of Europe's most extensive medieval city centres. The Barri Gòtic contains the cathedral and a maze of streets and squares.

SIGHTS AT A GLANCE

SEE ALSO

• *Street Life p29*

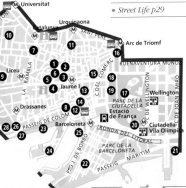

Decorated marble mailbox, Casa de l'Ardiaca

Casa de l'Ardiaca ❶

Map 4F. Carrer de Santa Llúcia. Open Mon–Sat except public hols. Free.

Standing beside what was originally the Bishop's Gate in the Roman wall is the Archdeacon's House. It was built in the 12th century, but its present form dates from around 1500 when it was remodelled, including the addition of a colonnade. In 1870 this was extended to form the Flamboyant Gothic patio around a fountain. Architect Domènech i Montaner (1850–1923) added the marble mailbox beside the portal. Upstairs are the City Archives.

Museu Frederic Marès ❷

Map 5F. Plaça de Sant Iu. Open daily Tue–Sun except. 1 Jan, Good Fri, 1 May, 25–26 Dec. Adm charge.

The sculptor Frederic Marès i Deulovol (1893–1991) was also a traveller and collector, and this museum is a monument to his eclectic taste. It is one of the most fascinating in

Virgin, Museu Frederic Marès

the city, and has an outstanding collection of Romanesque and Gothic religious art. Exhibits on the three floors range from clocks, crucifixes and costumes to antique cameras, pipes, tobacco jars and postcards. There is also a room full of children's toys.

Gothic nave of the Capella de Santa Àgata, Palau Reial

Museu d'Història de la Ciutat ❸

Map 5F. Plaça del Rei. Open daily Jun–Oct, and Tue–Sun Oct–May except 1 Jan, 1 May, 24 Jun, 25–26 Dec. Adm charge.

The Royal Palace was the residence of the count-kings of Barcelona in the 13th century. The complex includes the 14th-century Gothic Saló del Tinell, where Isabel and Fernando received Columbus after his return from America. It is also where the Holy Inquisition sat. Built into the Roman city wall is the royal chapel, the Capella de Santa Àgata, with a painted wood ceiling. Its bell tower is formed by part of a watch-

The magnificent council chamber, the Saló de Cent, in the Casa de la Ciutat

tower on the Roman wall. The main attraction of the Museu d'Història lies underground. Entire streets and squares of old Barcino are accessible via walkways suspended over the ruins of Roman Barcelona. They are the world's most extensive and complete subterranean Roman ruins in the world.

Casa de la Ciutat 4

Map 5E. Plaça de Sant Jaume. Open Sun or by appt. Free.

Flanking the entrance of the 14th-century city hall are statues of Jaume I, who granted the city rights to elect councillors in 1249, and Joan Fiveller, who levied taxes on court members. Inside is the 14th-century Saló de Cent, built for the city's 100 councillors.

Palau de la Generalitat 5

Map 5E. Plaça de Sant Jaume. Open 23 Apr, Sat by appt (call 93 402 46 17), 2nd, 4th Sun of every mth. Free.

Since 1403 the Generalitat has been the seat of the Catalonian government.

Above the entrance is a statue of Sant Jordi (St George) – patron saint of Catalonia – and the Dragon. The late Catalan-Gothic courtyard is by Marc Safont (1416). Among the fine interiors are the Gothic chapel of Sant Jordi and the Italianate Saló de Sant Jordi. The building is open to the public only on the saint's feast day. At the back lies the *Pati dels Tarongers*, the Orange Tree Patio, which has a bell tower built in 1568.

The Italianate façade of the Palau de la Generalitat

Cathedral 6

See pp16–17.

Barcelona Cathedral ❻

This compact Gothic cathedral was begun in 1298 under Jaume II but was not finished until the early 20th century, when the central spire was completed. A white marble choir screen, sculpted in the 16th century, depicts the martyrdom of St Eulàlia, the city's patron.

The Nave Interior *is Catalan-style Gothic, with 28 side chapels.*

The Main Façade *was not completed until 1889.*

Choir Stalls, *carved in the 15th-century, contain painted coats of arms.*

Sacristy Museum

VISITORS' CHECKLIST

Map 5F. Plaça de la Seu.
Tel 93 315 15 54. Open daily,
guided tours 1–5pm. Adm
charge except 8am–12.45pm
& 5.15–7.30pm daily. Sacristy
Museum open daily. Adm
charge. Choir daily. Adm
charge. Services daily.

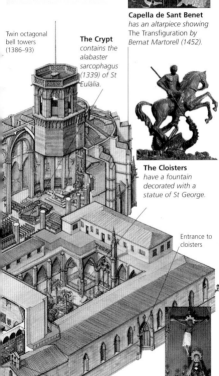

Capella de Sant Benet
*has an altarpiece showing
The Transfiguration by
Bernat Martorell (1452).*

**Twin octagonal
bell towers
(1386–93)**

The Crypt
*contains the
alabaster
sarcophagus
(1339) of St
Eulàlia.*

The Cloisters
*have a fountain
decorated with a
statue of St George.*

Entrance to
cloisters

Capella del Santíssim Sagrament
*is a small chapel housing the 16th-
century Christ of Lepanto crucifix.*

La Rambla 🟡

Map 4E.
Mercat de Sant Josep, Plaza de la
Boqueria: open Mon–Sat. Free.
Palau de la Virreina La Rambla:
open daily. Free.
Museu de Cera Pg de la Banca:
open daily. Times vary.
Adm charge.

The historic avenue of La
Rambla, leading to the sea,
is busy around the clock.
Newstands, caged bird and
flower stalls, musicians and
other entertainers throng the
wide, tree-shaded central
walkway. Among its famous
buildings are the Liceu
Opera House and the huge
Boqueria food market. The
name of this long avenue,
also known as Les Rambles,
comes from the Arabic
ramla, meaning the dried-
up bed of a seasonal river.
The 13th-century city wall

*The colourful pavement mosaic
by Catalan artist Joan Miró*

followed the left bank of
such a river that flowed
from the Collserola hills
to the sea.

Gran Teatre del Liceu

**Mercat de Sant
Josep** ⑤
*Also called "La
Boqueria", this is
Barcelona's most
colourful food
market.*

**Gran Teatre del
Liceu** ⑦
*Barcelona's opera
house.*

Palau Güell ⑨
*A Neo-Gothic
palace designed
by Gaudí
(see pp22–3).*

*The monument to
Columbus at the
bottom of the
tree-lined Rambla*

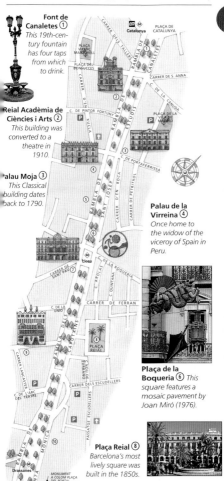

Font de Canaletes ①
This 19th-century fountain has four taps from which to drink.

Reial Acadèmia de Ciències i Arts ②
This building was converted to a theatre in 1910.

Palau Moja ③
This Classical building dates back to 1790.

Palau de la Virreina ④
Once home to the widow of the viceroy of Spain in Peru.

Plaça de la Boqueria ⑥ This square features a mosaic pavement by Joan Miró (1976).

Plaça Reial ⑧
Barcelona's most lively square was built in the 1850s.

Museu de Cera ⑩
This waxworks museum is housed in a 19th-century stately home.

0 metres 100
0 yards 100

Palau Güell **8**

See pp22–3.

El Raval **9**

Map 4D.

El Raval includes the old red-light area near the port. From the 14th century, the city hospital was in Carrer de l'Hospital, whch still has herbal and medicinal shops. The buildings now house the Biblioteca de Catalunya (Catalonian Library). Towards the port in Carrer Nou de la Rambla is Gaudí's Palau Güell (*see pp22–3*). At the end of Carrer Sant Pau is the 12th-century Romanesque church Sant Pau del Camp.

Museu d'Art Contemporani **10**

Map 4D. Plaça dels Angels. Open Mon, Wed–Sun, public hols except 25 Dec, 1 Jan. Adm charge.

This dramatic, glass-fronted building acts as the city's contemporary art mecca. The permanent collection of mainly Spanish painting,

sculpture and installation from the 1950s onwards is complemented by temporary exhibitions from foreign artists. Nearby is the Centre de Cultura Contemporània, which hosts major arts festivals and shows.

Stunning mosaic pillars, Palau de la Música Catalana

Palau de la Música Catalana **11**

Map 4F. Carrer de Sant Francesc de Paula. Open daily & for concerts. Adm charge.

This is a real palace of music, a Modernista celebra-

Façade of the Museu d'Art Contemporani

Glorious stained-glass dome, Palau de la Música Catalana

tion of tilework, sculpture and glorious stained glass. It is the only concert hall in Europe lit by natural light. Designed by Lluís Domènech i Montaner, it was completed in 1908. The elaborate red-brick façade is lined with mosaic-covered pillars topped by busts of the great composers. The large stone sculpture of St George and other figures at the corner of the building portrays an allegory from Catalan folksong by Miquel Blay. The auditorium is lit by a huge inverted dome of stained glass depicting angelic choristers. The stunning "Muses of the Palau", the group of 18 instrument-playing maidens, are the stage's backdrop. Made of terracotta and *trencadís* (broken pieces of ceramic) they have become the building's most admired feature. The Palau is being augmented by an underground concert hall and an outdoor square for summer concerts, consolidating its reputation as Barcelona's most loved music venue.

La Llotja ⑫

Map 5F. Carrer del Consolat de Mar. Closed to public.

La Llotja (meaning commodity exchange) was built in the 1380s as the headquarters of the Consolat de Mar. It was remodelled in Neo-Classical style in 1771 and housed the city's stock exchange until 1994. The upper floors housed the Barcelona School of Fine Arts from 1849 to 1970, attended by the young Picasso and Joan Miró.

Statue of Poseidon in the courtyard of La Llotja

Palau Güell ❽

Gaudí's first major work in Barcelona's city centre was commissioned by his patron Eusebi Güell. Finished in 1889, the house was used as a luxurious family home as well as a place to hold political meetings, chamber concerts and to put up important guests. High-quality materials were used: the stone work is clad with marble, and inside fine woods are featured.

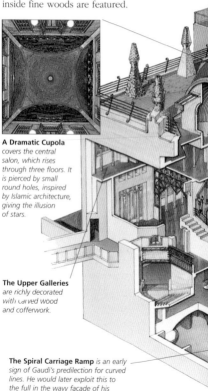

A Dramatic Cupola *covers the central salon, which rises through three floors. It is pierced by small round holes, inspired by Islamic architecture, giving the illusion of stars.*

The Upper Galleries *are richly decorated with carved wood and cofferwork.*

The Spiral Carriage Ramp *is an early sign of Gaudí's predilection for curved lines. He would later exploit this to the full in the wavy façade of his masterpiece, the Casa Milà (see p40).*

VISITORS' CHECKLIST

Map 5E. Nou de la Rambla.
Tel 93 317 39 74. Guided
tours available. Adm charge.
Closed until end 2006.

Ceramic Tiles
decorate the chimneys.

**Elaborate
Wrought Iron
Lamps** *light
the grand hall.*

Parabolic Arches,
*used extensively by
Gaudi, show his
interest in Gothic
architecture.*

An Escutcheon
*alludes to the
Catalan coat of arms.*

Museu Picasso

Map 5F. Carrer Montcada.
Open Tue–Sun, public hols
except 25–26 Dec, 1 Jan, Good
Fri, 1 May, 24 Jun. Adm charge
except 1st Sun of mth.

The Picasso Museum is
housed in medieval palaces
on Carrer Montcada: Berenguer d'Aguilar, Baró de
Castellet, Meca, Mauri and
Finestres. The museum
opened in 1963, and Picasso
himself donated paintings.
He also left graphic works
in his will. The strength of
the collection is Picasso's
early works: even at 15 and
16 years old he was painting
major works such as *The
First Communion* (1896)
and *Science and Charity*
(1897). There are only a few
pictures from his Blue and
Rose periods. The most
famous work is his series
Las Meninas, inspired by
Velázquez's masterpiece.

A wedding service in the Gothic
interior of Santa Maria del Mar

Basílica de Santa Maria del Mar

Map 5F. Pl Sta Maria. Open daily.
Free.

This beautiful building is the
only example of a church
entirely in the Catalan
Gothic style. It took just 55
years to build, with money
donated by merchants and
shipbuilders. The west front
has a 15th-century rose window of the Coronation of
the Virgin. More stained
glass, from the 15th to the
18th centuries, lights the
wide nave and high aisles.

Museu de la Xocolata

Map 5F. Comerç. Open Mon,
Wed–Sun, public hols except
25–26 Dec, 1 Jan, 1 May. Adm
charge except 1st Sun of mth.

The museum explores the
history of chocolate. This is
shown through old posters,
photographs and footage.
The real thing is displayed
in a homage to the art of the
mona, a traditional Catalan
Easter cake that evolved
over time into an edible
sculpture. A café serves delicious chocolate temptations.

Arc del Triomf

Map 4G. Passeig Lluís Companys.

The main gateway to the
1888 Universal Exhibition,
which filled the Parc de la
Ciutadella, was designed by
Josep Vilaseca i Casanovas.
It is built of brick in Mudéjar
(Spanish Moorish) style with
sculpted allegories of crafts,
industry and business. The
frieze on the main façade
represents the city welcom-
ing foreign visitors.

Parc de la Ciutadella

Map 5G. Avda del Marquès de
l'Argentera. Open daily. Free.

This popular park has a
boating lake, orange groves
and parrots living in the
palm trees. It was once the

site of a massive star-shaped citadel, built for Felipe V. In 1888 the park became the venue of the Universal Exhibition. On Sunday afternoons in particular people gather to play instruments, dance and relax, or visit the museums and zoo. Works by Catalan sculptors such as Mares, Arnau, Carbonell, Clara, Llimona, Gargallo, Dunyac and Fuxa can be seen in the park, alongside work by modern artists such as Tapies and Botero. A young Gaudí helped design the cascade and arch.

Hivernacle glasshouse, Museu de Geologia

Museu de Geologia **19**

Map 5G. Parc de la Ciutadella. Open Tue–Sun, public hols except 25–26 Dec, 1 Jan, Good Fri, 1 May. Adm charge.

Barcelona's oldest museum opened in 1882. This Neo-Classical building was the city's first public museum. Today, the museum boasts a large collection of fossils and minerals, including specimens from Catalonia.

Parc Zoològic **20**

Map 5G. Parc de la Ciutadella. Open daily. Adm charge.

This zoo was laid out in the 1940s to a relatively enlightened design – the animals are separated by moats instead of bars. Dolphin and whale shows are held in one of the aquariums. The zoo is very child-friendly and has pony rides, electric cars and a train.

One of the galleries inside the spacious Museu de Zoologia

Museu de Zoologia **18**

Map 5G. Passeig de Picasso. Open Tue–Sun & public hols. Adm charge.

This brick edifice was built by Lluís Domènech i Montaner for the 1888 Universal Exhibition. His inspiration was Valencia's Gothic commodities exchange. He later used it as a workshop for Modernista design, and it became a focus of the movement. It has housed the Zoologial Museum since 1937.

Children peering into an animal enclosure at the Parc Zoològic

Port Olímpic, with Spain's two tallest skyscrapers behind

Port Olímpic ㉑

Map 6H. Ciutadella-Vila Olímpica.

Developed for the 1992 Olympics, the project included 4 km (2 miles) of promenade and pristine sandy beaches and a 65-ha (160-acre) new estate of 2,000 apartments and parks called Nova Icària. On the sea front are twin 44-floor buildings, one offices, the other the Arts hotel. Port Olímpic itself has shops and nightclubs, but the main reasons for visiting are two levels of highly popular restaurants around the marina. Lunch can be walked off along the string of gently sloping beaches that is edged by a palm-fringed promenade with cafes.

Barceloneta ㉒

Map 6F.

Barcelona's fishing "village", which lies on a triangular tongue of land jutting into the sea just below the city centre, is renowned for its

restaurants and cafés. Its safe beach is also the closest to the city centre. In the small Plaça de la Barceloneta, at the centre of the district, is the Baroque church of Sant Miguel del Port. A market is often held in the square here. Today, Barceloneta's fishing fleet is still based in the nearby Moll del Rellotge (the clock dock), by a small clock tower. On the opposite side of this harbour is the Torre de Sant Sebastià, terminus of the cable car that runs right across the port to Montjuïc.

Fishing boat in Barceloneta harbour

Port Vell ㉓

Map 6E. Barceloneta.

Barcelona's marina is located at the foot of La Rambla (*see pp18–19*). The Moll d'Espanya boasts a vast new shopping and restaurant complex known as the Maremàgnum. Also on the Moll d'Espanya is an IMAX cinema and a large aquarium. On the shore, the Moll de Fusta (Timber Wharf), with terrace cafés, has red structures inspired by the bridge at Arles painted by Van Gogh. At the end of the wharf is El Cap de Barcelona (Barcelona Head), a 20-m (66-ft) tall

Maremàgnum shopping complex on the Moll d'Espanya, Port Vell

sculpture by artist Roy Lichtenstein. The Sports Marina on the other side of the Moll d'Espanya was once lined with warehouses. The only one left is now the Palau de Mar. Restaurants provide alfresco dining, but the building is otherwise given over to the Museu d'Història de Catalunya.

Aquarium ㉔

Map 6E. Moll d'Espanya. Open daily. Adm charge.

With over 11,000 organisms belonging to 450 species, Barcelona's aquarium is one of the biggest in Europe.

Spectacular glass viewing tunnel at the aquarium, Port Vell

The aquarium focuses particularly on the local Mediterranean coast. Highlights include moving platforms that ferry visitors through a glass tunnel under an "ocean" of sharks, rays and sunfish.

Café-lined façade of the Museu d'Història de Catalunya

Museu d'Història de Catalunya ㉕

Map 6F. Plaça Pau Vila. Open Tue–Sun, public hols. Adm charge except 1st Sun every mth.

This museum charts the history of Catalonia, from Lower Palaeolithic times through to the region's heydays as a maritime power and industrial pioneer. All captions are helpfully in Catalan, Spanish and English.

Monument a Colom ㉖

Map 6E. Plaça del Portal de la Pau. Open daily. Adm charge.

The Columbus monument was designed for the 1888 Universal Exhibition. The 60-m (200-ft) monument marks the spot where Columbus stepped ashore in 1493 after discovering America, bringing with him six Caribbean Indians. The Indians' conversion to Christianity is commemorated in the Cathedral (*see pp16–17*). A lift leads to a viewing platform at the top.

The Columbus Monument lit by fireworks during La Mercè fiesta

Golondrinas ㉗

Map 6E. Plaça del Portal de la Pau. Adm charge.

Sightseeing trips around Barcelona's harbour and to Port Olímpic can be made on *golondrinas* ("swallows") – small boats that moor in front of the Columbus Monument. They usually stop off at the breakwater, which reaches out to sea from Barceloneta, to allow passengers to disembark for a stroll.

A golondrina tour boat departing from the Portal de la Pau

Museu Marítim and Drassanes ㉘

Map 6D. Avinguda de les Drassanes. Open daily except 25–26 Dec, 1, 6 Jan. Adm charge.

The great galleys that helped make Barcelona a major seafaring power were built in the sheds of the shipyards that now house the maritime museum. These docks, founded in the mid-13th century, are the largest and most complete surviving medieval complex of their kind in the world. Three of the yard's four corner towers survive. Among the vessels to slip from the Drassanes' vaulted halls was the *Real*, flagship of Don Juan of Austria, who led the Christian fleet to victory against the Turks at Lepanto in 1571. The highlight of the museum's collection is a full-scale replica.

Stained-glass window in the Museu Marítim

STREET LIFE

RESTAURANTS AND TAPAS

Cal Pep
Map 5F. Pl de les Olles 8.
Tel 93 310 79 61.
Expensive
Tantalizing tapas, including the finest cured hams.

Txakolin
Map 5F. C/Marqués de l'Argentera 19.
Tel 93 268 17 81.
Moderate
Enjoy Basque-style tapas from cured ham to crab salad. The restaurant serves Basque fish and meat dishes.

El Xampanyet
Map 5F. C/Montcada 22.
Tel 93 319 70 03.
Moderate
Lively tapas bar serving champagne, cider and generous portions of tapas.

Egipte
Map 4E. La Rambla 79.
Tel 93 317 95 45.
Moderate
Boisterous diners pack this Modernista restaurant. Take your pick from 60 Catalan and Mediterranean dishes.

BARS AND CAFÉS

Café-Bar Jardin
Map 4E. C/Portaferrissa 17.
This lovely outdoor café, hidden upstairs at El Mercadillo, is shaded by trees and vine-covered walls.

Café-Bar L'Antiquari
Map 5F. C/Veguer 13.
In summer, bask in the old town's medieval atmosphere at the Plaça del Rei terrace. By night, sip Rioja in the intimate, rustic basement bodega.

Café del Born
Map 5F. Pl Comercial 10.
Plaça Comercial is dotted with cafés. This one evolves into an amiable bar as night descends.

Café d'Estiu
Map 5F. Pl de Sant Luc 5–6.
Tucked away on the patio of the Museu Frederic Marès is this alluring café, replete with stone pillars, climbing ivy and orange trees.

Xocoa
Map 4E. C/Petritxol 11.
This xocolateria has long been serving up goodies such as fig ravioli with peach ice-cream.

SHOPPING

Art Escudellers
Map 5E. C/Escudellers 23–25.
Vast array of colourful handmade Spanish ceramics. Also superb selection of Spanish wines and cured hams.

Atalanta Manufactura
Map 5E. Pg del Born 10.
Delicate, hand-painted silks created in an on-site workshop. Unusual designs include a Klimt-inspired, gilded silk.

La Manual Alpargatera
Map 5E. C/Avinyó 7.
What do Jack Nicholson and legions of Barcelonins have in common? They buy their espadrilles here.

Cereria Subirà
Map 5F. Baixada Llibreteria 7.
Founded in 1761, this is Barcelona's oldest shop. You'll find it crammed with every kind of candle imaginable.

See page 80 for price codes.

EIXAMPLE

Barcelona claims to have the greatest collection of Art Nouveau buildings of any city in Europe. The style, known in Catalonia as *Modernisme*, flourished after 1854, when the city was redeveloped. The designs of Idefons Cerdà i Sunyer were chosen for the new expansion (*eixample*) inland. The plans called for a rigid grid system of streets, but at each intersection the corners were chamfered to allow buildings to overlook the junctions or squares. Exceptions to this system include the Diagonal and the Hospital de la Santa Creu i de Sant Pau.

SIGHTS AT A GLANCE

Museums and Galleries
Fundació Antoni Tàpies ❸

Churches
Sagrada Família pp36–9 ❼

Modernista Buildings
Casa Batlló pp32–3 ❶
Casa Milà, "La Pedrera" ❹
Casa Terrades, "Casa de les Punxes" ❺

Hospital de la Santa Creu i de Sant Pau ❻
Mansana de la Discòrdia ❷

SEE ALSO

• *Street Life p41*

0 metres 500
0 yards 500

KEY

Ⓜ	Metro station
🚌	Main bus station
🚆	Train station
ℹ	Tourist Information

◀ *Nativity façade of the Sagrada Família*

Casa Batlló ❶

Unlike Gaudí's other works, this block of flats was a conversion of an existing building, completed in 1906. With its reworked façade in stunning organic forms and its fantastic chimneys and rooftop, it looks bold and convention-defying. The building has been said to symbolize St George killing the dragon, whose scaly back arches above the main façade.

The Attics
have white brick arches, giving the sensation of being inside the skeleton of an animal.

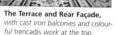

The Terrace and Rear Façade,
with cast iron balconies and colourful trencadís work at the top.

Dining room

Stairs to main floor

The Curved Iron Balconies *were pierced with holes to look like masks or skulls.*

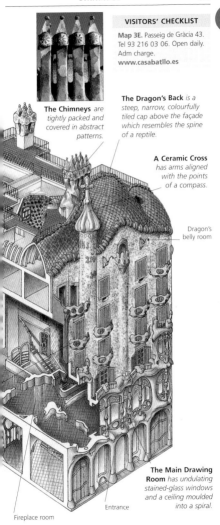

VISITORS' CHECKLIST

Map 3E. Passeig de Gràcia 43.
Tel 93 216 03 06. Open daily.
Adm charge.
www.casabatllo.es

The Chimneys are tightly packed and covered in abstract patterns.

The Dragon's Back is a steep, narrow, colourfully tiled cap above the façade which resembles the spine of a reptile.

A Ceramic Cross has arms aligned with the points of a compass.

Dragon's belly room

The Main Drawing Room has undulating stained-glass windows and a ceiling moulded into a spiral.

Entrance

Fireplace room

Casa Batlló ❶

See pp32–3.

Mansana de la Discòrdia ❷

Map 3E. Passeig de Gràcia, between Carrer d'Aragó and Carrer del Consell de Cent. **Centre del Modernisme** Casa Amatller, Passeig de Gràcia. Open daily. Free.

Barcelona's most famous group of Modernista buildings illustrates the range of styles used by the movement. They lie in an area known as the Mansana de la Discòrdia (Block of Discord), after the startling visual argument between them. The three finest were remodelled in Modernista style from existing houses early in the 20th century. No. 35 Passeig de Gràcia is Casa Lleó Morera (1902–6), the first residential work of Lluís Domènech i Montaner. A shop was installed in the ground floor, but the Modernista interiors upstairs still exist. Beyond the next two houses is Casa Amatller, designed by Puig i Cadafalch in 1898. The third house in the block is Antoni

Sumptuous interior of the Casa Lleó Morera, Mansana de la Discòrdia

Ornate tower gracing the Casa Lleó Morera, Mansana de la Discòrdia

Gaudí's Casa Batlló (*see pp32–3*) with its fluid façade evoking natural forms.

Fundació Antoni Tàpies **3**

Map 3E. Carrer d'Aragó. Open Tue–Sun & public hols except 25–26 Dec, 1, 6 Jan. Free to under 16s.

Antoni Tàpies, born in 1923, is Barcelona's best-known living artist. Inspired by

Surrealism, his abstract work is executed in a variety of materials, including concrete and metal. Difficult to appreciate at first, the exhibits should help viewers obtain a clearer perspective of Tàpies's work. The collection is in Barcelona's first domestic building to be constructed with iron (1880), designed by Domènech i Montaner for his brother's publishing firm.

This 1879 building houses a wide variety of Tàpies's work

ANTONI GAUDÍ (1852–1926)

Born in Reus (Tarragona) into an artisan family, Antoni Gaudí i Cornet was the leading exponent of Catalan Modernisme. After a blacksmith's apprenticeship, he studied at Barcelona's School of Architecture. Inspired by a nationalistic search for a romantic medieval past, his work was supremely original. His first major achievement was the Casa Vicens (1888) at No. 24 Carrer de les Carolines. But his most celebrated building is the church of the Sagrada Família (see pp36–9), to which he devoted his life from 1914. When he had put all his money into the project, he went from house to house begging for more. He was killed by a tram in 1926.

Decorated chimneypot, Casa Vicens

Sagrada Família ❼

Europe's most unconventional church, the Temple
Expiatori de la Sagrada Família is crammed with
symbolism. Gaudí was commissioned, in 1883, to
complete a Neo-Gothic cathedral. It became his
life's work and he lived like a recluse on the site
for 16 years. He is buried in the
crypt. Work continues today,
financed by public subscription.

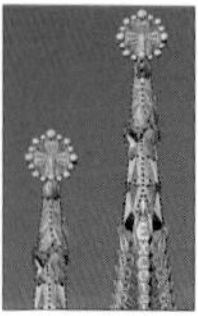

**The Bell
Towers** are
topped with
venetian
mosaics.

Tower
with lift

The Finished Church (below)
will include the central tower,
four large towers representing
the Evangelists and four
towers on the Glory
(south) façade.

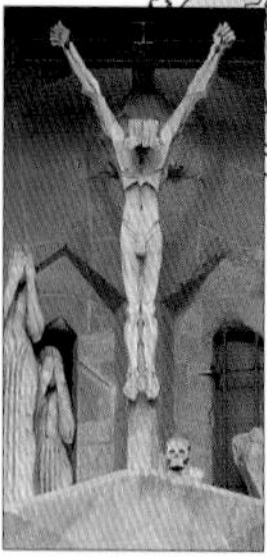

The
apse

Altar
canopy

The Passion Façade
was completed in the
late 1980s by artist
Josep Maria Subirachs.

Main entrance

Spiral staircases to towers and upper galleries

Tower with lift

VISITORS' CHECKLIST

Map 2H. C/ Mallorca.
Tel 93 207 30 31. Open daily
except 1, 6 Jan. Services daily.
Adm charge.
www.sagradafamilia.org

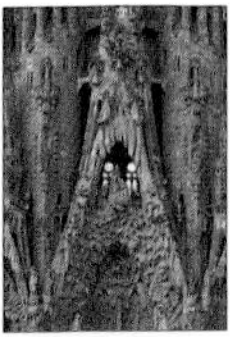

The Nativity Façade *has scenes of the Nativity and Christ's childhood.*

The Crypt, *where Gaudí is buried, was built by the original architect in 1882.*

Nave

Entrance to Crypt Museum

Passion Façade

It has been said that the Sagrada Família is meant to be perceived in the same way as a medieval cathedral, with each element representing a Biblical event or aspect of Christian faith. This was Gaudí's intent: his architecture was inseparable from the Catholicism which inspired it. The temple is dedicated to the Sagrada Família, the Holy Family. The two existing façades are detailed, visual accounts of two key Bible passages. The Glory façade will address the theme of judgement of sinners.

Main entrance, Passion façade

Christ's Passion

The Passion façade depicts the sufferings and execution of Jesus. The statuary has attracted criticism for its chunky, angular, "dehumanized" carving. A great porch shades the 12 groups of sculptures, arranged in three tiers. The first scene is the Last Supper. Next is the arrest in the Garden of Gethsemane. The kiss of betrayal by Judas follows.

The Flagellation

In the flagellation, Jesus is shown tied to a column at the top of a flight of three steps representing the three days of the Passion. Peter denying Christ is indicated

by the cock that will crow three times. Behind this group is a labyrinth, a metaphor for the loneliness of Jesus's path to the cross. The sculptural group on the bottom right includes Pilate washing his hands, freeing himself of responsibility for Jesus's death. Above, the "Three Marys" weep.

The Holy Shroud

The central sculpture depicts scenes from Jesus on the cross, including the solitary figure of the Roman centurion on horseback piercing the side of Jesus with his sword. The final scene is the burial of Jesus. The figure of Nicodemus, anointing the body, is thought to be a self-portrait of the sculptor Subirachs.

Knights sculpture, Passion façade

Nativity Façade

The northern, Nativity façade (overlooking Carrer Marina), finished according to Gaudí's personal instructions before his death, is far more subdued than the Passion façade: so much so that many of the sculptures barely rise out of the surface of the wall, making them difficult to identify. A great many natural forms are incorporated into the work, confusing interpretation further.

Faith, Hope and Charity

The ornamentation of the façade is arranged around three doors dedicated to Hope, Faith and Charity or Christian Love. Various animal symbols represent the permanence and stability of Christianity and the forces of change. Four angels call to the four winds and announce the proximity of the end of the world.

Hope Doorway

The lowest carvings of the Hope Doorway show the Flight into Egypt and the Slaughter of the Innocents. There are also representations of Jesus's parents and grandparents. Above the doorway is an allusion to the holy Catalan mountain of Montserrat.

Faith Doorway

The Faith Doorway illustrates passages from the gospels and Christian theology. The heart of Jesus can be seen set into the lintel above the door. A scene depicts the Visitation by Mary to Elizabeth, her cousin and mother of John the Baptist. Another scene

Detail of sculpture, Nativity façade

has Jesus wielding a hammer and chisel in his father's workshop.

Charity Doorway

The double doors of the central Charity Doorway are separated by a column recording Jesus's genealogy. The three magi are on the lower left of the door with the shepherds opposite them. Out of the nativity emerges a many-pointed star (or comet). Above the star is the Annunciation and the Coronation of the Virgin Mary by Jesus.

The rippled façade of Gaudí's apartment building, Casa Milà

Casa Milà ❹

Map 2F. Passeig de Gràcia. Open daily except 25–26 Dec, 1, 6 Jan. Adm charge.

Usually called *La Pedrera* (the Stone Quarry), the Casa Milà is Gaudí's greatest contribution to Barcelona's civic architecture, and his last work before he devoted himself to the Sagrada Família (*see pp36–9*). Built between 1906–10, La Pedrera departed from established construction principles and was ridiculed by Barcelona's intellectuals. Gaudí designed his eight-floor apartment block around two circular courtyards. It features the city's first underground car park. The ironwork balconies, by Josep Maria Jujol, are like seaweed against the wave-like walls of white stone. There are no straight walls anywhere in the building. The Milà family had an apartment on the first floor, which now features a typical Modernista interior. The museum, "El Espai Gaudí", on the top floor, includes models and explanations of Gaudí's work. From here, visitors can access the roof. The sculptured ducts and chimneys have a such a threatening appearance that they are known as *espanta-bruixes*, or witch-scarers.

Casa Terrades ❺

Map 2F. Avinguda Diagonal. Not open to the public.

This free-stand-ing, six-sided apartment block by Modernista architect Josep Puig i Cadafalch gets its nickname, *Casa de les Punxes* (House of the Points), from the spires on its corner turrets.

Spire on the main tower, Casa Terrades

Built between 1903 and 1905 it is an eclectic mix of medieval, Renaissance and Modernista styles.

Hospital de la Santa Creu i de Sant Pau **6**

Map 1J. Carrer de Sant Antoni Maria Claret. Grounds open daily. Free.

Lluís Domènech i Montaner began designing a new city hospital in 1902. Based on 26 Mudéjar-style pavilions set in gardens, he believed that patients would recover better among fresh air and

trees. All the connecting corridors and service areas were underground.

Sagrada Família **7**

See pp36–9.

Statue of the Virgin, Hospital de la Santa Creu i de Sant Pau

STREET LIFE

RESTAURANTS AND TAPAS

La Semproniana
Map 2E. C/Rosselló 148.
Tel 93 453 18 20.
Moderate
Set in an old printworks, the food is a cross between Catalan and nouvelle cuisine.

Qu Qu
Map 3F. Pg de Gràcia 24.
Tel 93 317 45 12.
Cheap
Hugely popular tapas. Try the three-cheese croquettes.

La Principal
Map 2E. C/Provença 286.
Tel 93 272 08 45.
Moderate
Oriental in design with a great terrace and "new" Mediterranean food.

CAFÉS

Laie Llibreria Cafè
Map 4F. C/Pau Claris 85.
A cultural meeting place with a lively atmosphere. There's an excellent set lunch and live jazz (Mar–May: Tue).

Cafè del Centre
Map 3F. C/Girona 69.
The Eixample's oldest café.

La Botiga del Te i Cafè
Map 3E. Pl Dr Letamendi 30–33.
Specialist café with more than 50 types of tea and coffee.

Hotel Ritz
Map 3F. Gran Via de les Corts Catalanes 668.
Perfect for breakfast or afternoon tea.

SHOPPING

Vinçon
Map 2F. Pg de Gràcia 96.
Out-of-this-world designs for the most everyday objects.

Dos i Una
Map 2F. C/Rosselló 275.
Gift shop selling unusual "made in Barcelona" items.

Regia
Map 2E. Pg de Gràcia 39.
Over 1,000 perfumes on sale.

See page 80 for price codes.

MONTJUÏC

Montjuïc, rising to 213 m (699 ft) above the port on the south side of the city, is Barcelona's biggest recreation area, with museums, art galleries, gardens and nightclubs. In the middle of the Avinguda de la Reina Cristina is the Font Màgica (Magic Fountain). Above it, in the Palau Nacional, are the city's historic art collections.

SIGHTS AT A GLANCE

Historic Buildings
Castell de Montjuïc **7**

Modern Architecture
Estadi Olímpic de
   Montjuïc **8**
Pavelló Mies van der
   Rohe **4**

Museums and Galleries
Fundació Joan Miró **1**
Museu Arqueològic **2**

Museu Nacional d'Art de
   Catalunya **3**

Squares
Plaça d'Espanya **6**

Theme Parks
Poble Espanyol **5**

SEE ALSO

* *Street Life p47*

KEY

Ⓜ Metro station

🚠 Funicular station

🚡 Cable car station

Ⓖ FGC station

◀ *Changing colours of the Font Màgica (Magic Fountain)*

Colourful sculptures on the terrace at the Fundació Joan Miró

Fundació Joan Miró ❶

Map 5B. Parc de Montjuïc. Open daily except 25–26 Dec, 1 Jan. Adm charge.

Joan Miró (1893–1983) went to La Llotja's art school (*see p21*), but from 1919 spent much time in Paris. Though opposed to Franco, he returned to Spain in 1940 and lived mainly in Mallorca, where he died. An admirer of Catalan art and Modernisme, Miró remained a Catalan painter but invented and developed a Surrealistic style, with vivid colours and fantastical forms. During the 1950s he concentrated on ceramics. In 1975, after the return of democracy to Spain, his friend, the architect Josep Lluís Sert, designed this stark, white building to house a permanent collection of graphics, paintings, sculptures and tapestries lit by natural light. Miró himself donated the works and some of the best pieces on display include his *Barcelona Series* (1939–44), a set of 50 black-and-white lithographs. Exhibitions of other artists' work are also held regularly.

Museu Arqueològic ❷

Map 5B. Passeig Santa Madrona. Open Tue–Sun, public hols except 25–26 Dec, 1 Jan. Adm charge except 11 Feb, 23 Apr, 18 May, 11, 24 Sep.

Housed in the 1929 Palace of Graphic Arts, the museum has artifacts from prehistory to the Visigothic period (AD 415–711). Highlights are finds from the Greco-Roman town of Empúries (*see pp62–3*), Hellenistic Mallorcan and Visigothic jewellery and Iberian silver treasure.

Dama d'Evissa, a sculpture in the Museu Arqueològic

Museu Nacional d'Art de Catalunya ❸

Map 4B. Parc de Montjuïc, Palau Nacional. Open Tue–Sun, public hols except 25–26 Dec, 1 Jan, 1 May. Adm charge except 1st Thu of mth.

The austere Palau Nacional was built for the 1929 International Exhibition, but since 1934, it has housed the city's most important art collection. The Museu Nacional d'Art de Catalunya has probably the greatest display of Romanesque items to be found anywhere in the world, centred around a series of magnificent 12th-century frescoes. The most remarkable are the wall paintings from Sant Climent de Taüll and Santa Maria de de Taüll. There is also an expanding Gothic collection. Notable artists include the 15th-century Spanish artists Lluís Dalmau and Jaume Huguet. Works by El Greco, Zurbarán and Velázquez are on display in the Cambó rooms, a collection of notable Baroque and Renaissance works from all over Europe. The musem has recently expanded and now houses the entire body of 20th-century art, furniture and sculpture previously at the Museu d'Art Modern in the Parc de la Ciutadella. It also houses the Thyssen-Bornemisza collection, with works by Tiepolo, Titian, Lotto, Canaletto and Velázquez.

Barcelona Chairs, *Pavelló Mies van der Rohe*

Pavelló Mies van der Rohe ❹

Map 4B. Avinguda del Marquès de Comillas. Open daily except 25 Dec, 1 Jan. Free to under 18s.

If the simple lines of this glass and polished stone pavilion look modern today, they must have shocked visitors at the 1929 International Exhibition. Designed by Ludwig Mies van der Rohe (1886–1969), director of the Bauhaus school, it included his world-famous *Barcelona Chair*.

The Museu Nacional d'Art de Catalunya houses Europe's finest collection of Romanesque frescoes

Poble Espanyol ❺

Map 4A. Avinguda del Marquès de Comillas. Open daily. Adm charge.

The Poble Espanyol (Spanish Village) was laid out for the 1929 International Exhibition, but has proved to be enduringly popular. Building styles from all over Spain are illustrated by 116 houses, arranged on streets radiating from a main square. The village was refurbished at the end of the 1980s. Resident artisans produce crafts including hand-blown glass, ceramics, Toledo damascene and Catalan sandals (*espardenyes*). Other attractions include shops, bars and a children's theatre.

Looking down from the Palau Nacional towards Plaça d'Espanya

Plaça d'Espanya ❻

Map 3B. Avinguda de la Gran Via de les Corts Catalanes.

The fountain in the middle of this road junction is by Josep Maria Jujol. The sculptures are by Miquel Blay. The 1899 bullring to one side is by Font i Carreras, but Catalans have never taken to bullfighting. On the Montjuïc side of the roundabout is the Avinguda de la Reina Maria Cristina. This is flanked by two 47-m (154-ft) high brick campaniles, modelled on the bell towers of St Mark's in Venice and built as the entrance way to the 1929 International Exhibition. The avenue, lined with exhibition buildings, leads to Carles Buigas's illuminated Font Magica (Magic Fountain) in front of the Palau Nacional.

Castell de Montjuïc ❼

Map 6B. Parc de Montjuïc. Museum open daily except 25–26 Dec, 1 Jan, Good Fri, 1 May. Adm charge.

The summit of Montjuïc is occupied by a huge, 18th-century castle with views

Poble Espanyol contains replicas of buildings from many regions of Spain

Castell de Montjuïc

over the port. It is now a military museum displaying ancient weaponry and model castles.

Estadi Olímpic de Montjuïc **8**

Map 5B. Passeig Olímpic, S/N. Open daily except 25 Dec, 1 Jan. Free.

The original Neo-Classical façade has been preserved from the stadium built by Pere Domènech i Roura for the 1936 Olympics, which was cancelled at the onset of the Spanish Civil War. The arena's capacity was raised to 70,000 for the 1992 Olympics. Nearby are the steel-and-glass Palau Sant Jordi stadium by Japanese architect Arata Isozaki, and swimming pools by Ricard Bofill.

Estadi Olímpic de Montjuïc

STREET LIFE

RESTAURANTS

MNAC Restaurant
Map 4B. Parc de Montjuïc.
Tel 93 424 21 92.
Moderate
The grand Oval Room of the Palau Nacional has specialities including vegetables au gratin.

Cañota
Map 4C. C/Lleida 7.
Tel 93 325 91 71.
Moderate
Traditional cooking includes excellent game dishes.

Fundació Joan Miró Restaurant
Map 5B. Parc de Montjuïc.
Tel 93 329 07 68.
Moderate
A large terrace, views of Miró's sculptures, plus modern, Italian-style food.

L'Albi
Map 4A. Poble Espanyol.
Tel 93 424 93 24.
Moderate
This restaurant offers stunning views and traditional Mediterranean dishes.

Font de Prades
Map 4A. Poble Espanyol.
Tel 93 426 75 19.
Expensive
By far the best food in the Poble Espanyol, with tables scattered around a courtyard.

BARS

Bar Miramar
Map 6C. Av de Miramar.
No prizes for the chicken-and-chips style cuisine, but this bar has great city panoramas.

See page 80 for price codes.

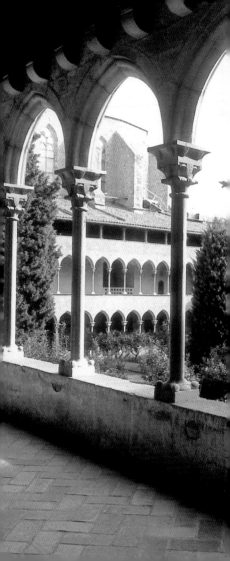

FURTHER AFIELD

Redevelopments in the 1980s and 1990s have
given Barcelona new buildings, parks and
squares, including Parc de l'Espanya Industrial
and Parc de Joan Miró. There is a new national
theatre in the east and the royal palace and
monastery of Pedralbes and Torre Bellesguard in
the west. Tibidabo is popular for a day out.

SIGHTS AT A GLANCE

Museums and Galleries
CaixaForum **12**
CosmoCaixa **9**
Museu del Futbol Club
   Barcelona **3**

Historic Buildings
Monestir de Santa Maria de
   Pedralbes **4**
Palau Reial de Pedralbes **5**
Torre Bellesguard **10**

Modern Buildings
Torre de Collserola **6**

Parks and Gardens
Parc de l'Espanya
   Industrial **2**
Parc Güell pp 52–3 **7**
Parc de Joan Miró **1**
Parc del Laberint d'Horta **11**

Squares and Districts
Estació del Nord **13**
Plaça de les Glòries
   Catalanes **14**
Poblenou **15**

Theme Parks
Tibidabo **8**

KEY

🚇 Train station

🚋 Tram stop

0 km   2

0 miles   2

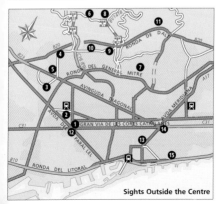

Sights Outside the Centre

◀ *The cloister at the outstandingly beautiful Monestir de Pedralbes*

Parc de Joan Miró ❶

Carrer d'Aragó. Free.

Barcelona's 19th-century slaughterhouse was transformed in the 1980s into an unusual park. It is on two levels, the lower of which is devoted to football pitches and areas of trees and flowers. The upper level has a sculpture by Catalan artist Joan Miró entitled *Dona i Ocell* (Woman and Bird).

Parc de Joan Miró

Parc de l'Espanya Industrial ❷

Plaça de Joan Peiró. Free.

This park owes its name to the textile mill that stood on the site. The park has canals and a rowing lake. Steps rise around the lake like an amphitheatre, and ten futur-

Line of watchtowers in the Parc de l'Espanya Industrial

istic watchtowers dominate the area. Six contemporary sculptors are represented in the park, including Andrés Nagel, whose metal dragon incorporates a slide.

Museu del Futbol Club Barcelona ❸

Avda de Arístides Maillol. Open daily except 24–25 Dec, 1, 6 Jan. Adm charge.

Camp Nou, Europe's largest football stadium, is home to the city's football club, Barcelona FC. The sweeping stadium seats 100,000. The club's museum displays memorabilia and trophies, and has a souvenir shop.

View across Camp Nou stadium

Monestir de Santa Maria de Pedralbes

Monestir de Santa Maria de Pedralbes ❹

Carrer de Montevideo. Open Tue–Sun except public hols. Adm charge.

The monastery of Pedralbes was founded in 1326, and is built around a three-story cloister. The main rooms include a dormitory, a refectory, a chapterhouse, an abbey and day cells. Works of art, as well as liturgical oranaments, are on display. The most important room is the Capella (chapel) de Sant Miquel, with murals of the *Passion* and the *Life of the Virgin*, both painted by Ferrer Bassa in 1346.

Palau Reial de Pedralbes ❺

Avda Diagonal. Museu de Ceràmica & Museu de Arts Decoratives open Tue–Sun, public hols except 25–26 Dec, 1 Jan, 1, 20 May, 24 Jun. Adm charge except 1st Sun of mth.

The Palace of Pedralbes incorporates the Museu de Arts Decoratives, whose exhibits include furniture and household items from the Middle Ages to the present. The palace also houses the Museu de Ceràmica, which displays pottery and ceramics, including works by Miró and Picasso.

Torre de Collserola ❻

Carretera de Vallvidrera al Tibidabo. Open Wed–Sun except 25 Dec, 1, 6 Jan. Adm charge.

The 288-m (944-ft) tall tower was designed for the 1992 Olympic Games. There are 13 levels. The top one has an observatory with a telescope and a platform offering panoramic views.

Parc Güell ❼

See pp52–3.

Tibidabo ❽

Plaça del Tibidabo. Amusement Park: tel 93 211 79 42 for opening times. Temple Expiatori del Sagrat Cor open daily. Free.

Tibidabo can be reached by Barcelona's last surviving tram. The Parc d'Atraccions (Amusement Park) includes the Museu d'Autòmats, with automated toys, juke boxes and slot machines. Tibidabo is topped by the Temple Expiatori del Sagrat Cor.

Merry-go-round, Tibidabo

Parc Güell ➐

In 1910 Eusebio Güell commissioned Gaudí to lay out a private housing estate on a hillside above Barcelona. The plan was to create a mini garden city, but only two of the houses were built. The layout is loosely based on the Sanctuary of Apollo at Delhi and includes arcades and viaducts by Gaudí and mosaics by Josep Maria Jujol.

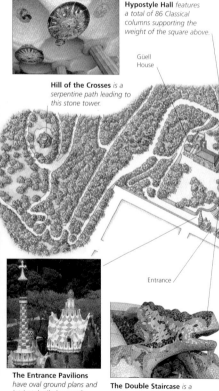

Hypostyle Hall *features a total of 86 Classical columns supporting the weight of the square above.*

Güell House

Hill of the Crosses *is a serpentine path leading to this stone tower.*

Entrance

The Entrance Pavilions *have oval ground plans and intricately tiled* trencadis *exteriors.*

The Double Staircase *is a monumental flight of steps topped by an emblematic dragon.*

The Square *has a serpentine bench covered in trencadis that curves all the way around the edge.*

VISITORS' CHECKLIST

Olot, Vallcarca. Open daily.
Tel 93 285 68 99 .
Casa-Museu Gaudí open
daily. Tel 93 219 38 11.
Adm charge.
www.bcn.es/parcsijardins

The Trias House *is one of only two houses to have been built in the planned housing estate.*

The Upper Viaduct *is one of three that carry snaking pathways on the east side of the park.*

Perimeter wall

Casa-Museu Gaudí *contains furniture designed by Gaudí.*

CosmoCaixa 9

Teodor Roviralta. Open Tue–Sun.
Adm charge.

Barcelona's stimulating and
interactive science museum
now has a new wing on
nine levels. Its particular
boast is a glasshouse
containing a recreated sec-
tion of a flooded Amazon
forest, inhabited by animal
and plant species. Other
exhibition spaces include
the Matter Room, which
looks at the big bang theory.

Torre Bellesguard 10

Carrer de Bellesguard. Not open
to the public.

Here, half way up the
Collserola hills, is where
medieval Catalan kings had
their summer home. In 1900
Gaudí built the present
house on the site of the castle. Its castellated look and
the Gothic-inspired win-
dows refer to the original
castle. Gaudí kept the ves-
tiges of its walls in his structure. The roof, with a walkway behind the parapet, is
topped by a Gaudí tower.

*Wrought-iron entrance door at
Antoni Gaudí's Torre Bellesguard*

Parc del Laberint d'Horta 11

Germans Desvalls, Passeig
Castanyers. Open daily. Adm
charge except Wed, Sun.

The centrepiece of the city's
oldest public park, created
in the 18th century, is a
cypress maze. The semi-
wild garden slopes steeply
uphill from the entrance
beside a semi-derelict
palace which now houses
a gardening school. It is a
compendium of aristocratic
Baroque fantasies. Classical
temples dedicated to
Ariadne and Danae stand at
either side of a broad paseo
which oversees the maze.
From here, steps leads up
to a Neo-Classical temple.
Elsewhere there is a "romantic garden", a faux cemetery
and, in the woodland into
which the garden eventually
leads, a hermit's cave.

CaixaForum 12

Avinguda del Marquès de
Comillas, Montjuïc. Open
Tue–Sun. Free.

The "la Caixa" Foundation's
collection of 700 works by
Spanish and international
artists is housed in the
Antiga Fàbrica Casaramona,
a restored Mondernista-style
textile mill built by Josep
Puig i Cadafalch. Opened in
1911, it was intended to be
a model factory but closed
down in 1920. The collec-
tion is displayed according
to changing themes, but one
permanent exhibit is Joseph
Beuy's *Lead Room
(Chamber of Pain)*. There
are also temporary art
exhibitions.

Blue-tiled sculpture by Beverley Pepper, Parc de l'Estació del Nord

Estació del Nord ⑬

Avinguda de Vilanova. Free.

Only the 1861 façade and the grand 1915 entrance remain of this former railway station. The rest has been remodelled as a sports centre, a police headquarters and the city's bus station. Two elegant, blue-tiled sculptures, *Espiral arbrada (Branched Spiral)* and *Cel obert (Open Sky)* by Beverley Pepper (1992) sweep through the park.

Plaça de les Glòries Catalanes ⑭

Gran Via de les Corts Catalanes.

This whole area, where the Diagonal crosses the Gran Via de les Corts Catalanes, has recently been redeveloped, completing the vision of the Eixample's planner Ildefons Cerdà. On the north side, a new shopping centre contrasts with the Encants Vells flea market, which sprawls beside the highway heading north out of town. To the south of the plaça is the new Teatre Nacional de Catalunya, a vast temple to culture by architect Ricard Bofill. Beside it is the Auditori de Barcelona, with two concert

halls by Rafael Moneo which were inaugurated in 1999.

Catalonia's National Theatre near the Plaça de les Glòries Catalanes

Poblenou ⑮

Rambla del Poblenou.

In Poblenou artists have built studios in the defunct warehouses of the city's former industrial heartland. The area is centred on the Rambla del Poblenou, extending from Avinguda Diagonal down to the sea. In the streets leading from the Rambla are a few protected pieces of industrial architecture. Along the parallel Carrer del Ferrocarril is the Plaça de Prim, reminiscent of a country town.

La Rambla del Poblenou

Palau de *la* Música Catalana ▶

DAY TRIPS IN CATALONIA

Catalonia is a region of varied scenery and a wealth of attractions. It includes a long stretch of the Spanish Pyrenees, whose green, flower-filled valleys hide picturesque villages with Romanesque churches. The south and eastern coastal region is perfect for sun-lovers. Visitors can choose between the rugged Costa Brava or the long sandy stretches of the Costa Daurada. Tarragona is rich in Roman monuments. Inland there are famous monasteries such as Poblet and Santes Creus.

SIGHTS AT A GLANCE

KEY	
✈	Airport

| 0 km | 40 |
| 0 miles | 40 |

◀ *Inner courtyard, Monestir de Montserrat*

Girona ❶

Market: Tue, Sat. Festivals: El
Pedal (bike race, last fortnight
Sept, Sant Narci (29 Sep for a wk)

Girona's best face is beside
the Riu Onyar, where pastel-
coloured buildings rise
above the water. Behind
them, the Rambla de la
Llibertat is lined with shops
and street cafés. The best
way to see the town's ram-
parts, first raised by the
Romans, is to take the
Passeig Arqueològic
(Archaeological Walk). The
walk's starting point is on
the north side of the town,
near the **Església de Sant**

Pere de Galligants. The
church houses the city's
archaeological collection.
From here, a narrow street
goes through the north gate,
where Roman foundation
stones are visible. They
mark the route from
Tarragona (*see p71*) to
Rome. The most popular
place of devotion in the
town is the **Església de
Sant Feliu**, built over the
tombs of St Felix and St
Narcissus, both patrons of
the city. Despite their name,
the nearby **Banys Àrabs**
(Arab Baths) were built
about 300 years after the
Moors had left.

GIRONA TOWN CENTRE

Painted houses packed tightly along the bank of the Riu Onyar in Girona

Catedral

Girona Cathedral's nave has the widest Gothic span in the Christian world. The cathedral museum's most famous item is a tapestry, *The Creation*.

Museu d'Art

Pujada de la Catedral. Open daily except 25–26 Dec, 1, 6 Jan. Adm charge.

This gallery holds works from the Romanesque period to the 20th century.

Museu d'Història de la Ciutat

Carrer de la Força. Open Tue–Sun except 25–26 Dec, 1, 6 Jan. Free.

The history museum is in an 18th-century former convent. Exhibits include old *sardana* instruments.

Centre Bonastruc Ça Porta

Carrer de la Força. Open daily except 25–26 Dec, 1, 6 Jan. Adm charge.

The centre charts the history of Girona's Jews. The buildings it occupies were once part of El Call, the Jewish

ghetto – inhabited by the city's Jews from the late 9th century until their expulsion from Spain in 1492.

Figueres ❷

Tapestry of The Creation

Market: Thu. Festivals: Santa Creu (3 May), Sant Pere (29 Jun). Museu del Joguet (Toy Museum) open Tue–Sun. Adm charge. Teatre-Museu Dalí open Tue–Sun except 25 Dec, 1 Jan. Adm charge. Casa-Museu Castell Gala Dalí open Tue–Sun. Adm charge.

Figueres is the market town of the Empordà plain. It was the birthplace of Salvador Dalí (1904–1989), the best-known exponent of Surrealism, who turned the town theatre into the Teatre-Museu Dalí. Under its glass dome are works by Dalí and other painters. The museum is a monument to Catalonia's most eccentric artist. The Casa-Museu Castell Gala Dalí, 55 km (35 miles) south of Figueres, is the medieval castle Dalí bought in the 1970s. It contains some of his paintings. East of Figueres is the Romanesque monastery, Sant Pere de Rodes.

Cadaqués has small, unspoilt stony beaches and an arty atmosphere

Cadaqués ❸

Girona. Market: Mon. Festivals:
Fiesta major de Verano (1st wk
Sep), Santa Esperança (18 Dec).

This pretty resort is over-
looked by the Baroque
Església de Santa Maria. In
the 1960s it was dubbed the
"St Tropez of Spain", due to
the young crowd that
sought out Salvador Dalí in
nearby Port Lligat. For six
months of the year, from
1930 until his death in 1989,
Dalí lived here with his wife
Gala. Today their much
modified house, which
expanded far beyond their
original fisherman's cabin,
is known as the Casa-Museu
Salvador Dalí. Managed by
the Gala-Salvador Dalí
Foundation, the museum
and its contents provide a
unique interpretation of the
artist's life and inspiration.

Empúries ❹

Girona. Open daily Easter,
Jun–Sep. Adm charge to ruins.

The extensive ruins of this
Greco-Roman town occupy
an imposing site beside the
sea. Three separate settle-
ments were built between
the 7th and 3rd centuries
BC: the old town (Palaia-
polis); the new town
(Neapolis); and the Roman
town. The old town was
founded by the Greeks in
600 BC as a trading port.
It was built on what was a
small island, and is now the
site of the tiny hamlet of
Sant Martí de Empúries. In
550 BC this was replaced by
a larger new town on the
shore which the Greeks
named Emporion, meaning
"trading place". In 218 BC,
the Romans landed at
Empúries and built a city
next to the new town. A
nearby museum exhibits
some of the site's finds, but

*An excavated Roman pillar in the
ruins of Empúries*

the best are in Barcelona's Museu Arqueològic (*see p44*).

Peratallada **5**

Girona. Festivals: Feria Peratallada (last wknd Apr), Festa Major (6–7 Aug), Medieval Market (1st wknd Oct).

This tiny village is the most spectacular of the many that lie a short inland trip from the Costa Brava. Together with Pals and Palau Sator, it forms part of the "Golden Triangle" of medieval villages. Its mountain-top position gives some dramatic views of the area. A labyrinth of cobbled streets wind up to the well-con-served castle and look out tower, whose written records date from the 11th century. Peratallada's counts and kings made doubly sure of fending off any attackers by constructing a sturdy wall enclosing the entire village that even today limits the nucleus from fur-ther expansion, ensuring the village retains its medieval character.

Tossa de Mar **6**

Girona. Market: Thu. Festivals: Festa de hivern (22 Jan), Festa d estiu (29 Jun). Museu Municipal open daily. Adm charge.

At the end of a tortuous cor-niche, the Roman town of Turissa is one of the pretti-est along the Costa Brava. Above the modern town is the Vila Vella (old town), a protected national monu-ment. The medieval walls enclose fishermen's cot-tages, a 14th-century church

Looking south along the Costa Brava from Tossa de Mar

and countless bars. The Museu Municipal in the old town exhibits local archaeo-logy and modern art.

Blanes **7**

Girona. Market: Mon. Festivals: Santa Ana (26 Jul), Festa Major Petita (21 Aug).

The working port of Blanes has one of the longest beaches on the Costa Brava. The highlight of the town is the Jardí Botànic Mar i Murtra. These gardens, designed by Karl Faust in 1928, are spectacularly sited above cliffs. Their 7,000 species of Mediterranean and tropical plants include African cacti.

The Costa Brava has a rich underwater fauna and flora

Monestir de Montserrat ⑧

The "serrated mountain" (*mont serrat*), its highest peak rising to 1,236 m (4,055 ft), is the setting for Catalonia's holiest place, the Monastery of Montserrat. The monastery was first mentioned in the 9th century. It was destroyed in 1811. Rebuilt and repopulated in 1844, it is occupied by Benedictine monks.

Benedictine monk

Plaça de Santa Maria has a façade by Francesc Folguera.

The Way of the Cross passes 14 statues depicting the Stations of the Cross.

Museum

Gothic cloister

Funicular to holy site of Santa Cova

The Basilica Façade
is Neo-Renaissance, and
replaces the Plateresque
façade of the original
church.

VISITORS' CHECKLIST

Montserrat (Barcelona
province). Tel 93 877 77 75.
Basilica open daily. Services
9am Mon–Fri, 7.30am Sat,
8am Sun & religious hols.
Museum open daily.
Adm charge.
www.abadiamontserrat.net

The Black Virgin, a small wooden
statue of La Moreneta (the dark
maiden) is said to have been made
by St Luke and brought here
by St Peter in AD 50. In
1881 Montserrat's Black
Virgin became patroness
of Catalonia.

The Basilica Interior
has an enamelled altar
and paintings.

The Inner Courtyard
contains the baptistry
(1902), with sculptures
by Carles Collet.

Rack
railway

Cable car to Aeri de
Montserrat station

Twelfth-century altar frontal, Museu Episcopal de Vic

Vic ❾

Barcelona. Market: Tue, Sat. Festivals: Mercat del Ram (Sat before Easter), Sant Miquel (5–15 Jul), Música Viva (3 days mid-Sep), Mercat medieval (6–8 Dec). Museu Episcopal de Vic open Tue–Sun except 25–26 Dec, 1, 6 Jan. Adm charge.

Market days are the best time to go to this town. In the 11th century, Abbot Oliva commissioned El Cloquer tower, around which the cathedral was built in the 18th century. The interior has murals of Biblical scenes. Adjacent to the cathedral is the Museu Episcopal de Vic, which has one of the best Romanesque collections in Catalonia.

Cardona ❿

Barcelona. Market: Sun. Festivals: Carnival (Feb), Festa major (2nd Sun of Sep).

This 13th-century castle of the Dukes of Cardona, constables to the crown of Aragón, is set on the top of a hill. The castle was rebuilt in the 18th century. Beside

the castle is an elegant 11th-century church.

Solsona ⓫

Lleida. Market: Tue, Fri. Festivals: Carnival (Feb), Sant Isidro (closest weekend to 15 May), Corpus Christi (May/Jun), Festa major (8–11 Sep). Museu Diocesà i Comarcal open Tue–Sun except 25–26 Dec, 1 Jan. Free. Museu del Ganivet open Tue–Sun except 25–26 Dec, 6 Jan. Adm charge.

Nine towers and three gateways remain of Solsona's fortifications. Inside is an ancient town of noble mansions. The cathedral houses a black stone Virgin. The Museu Diocesà i Comarcal has Romanesque paintings and the Museu Ganivets has a fine knife collection.

Lleida ⓬

Lleida. Market: Thu, Sat. Festivals: Sant Anastasi (11 May), Sant Miquel (29 Sep).

Dominating Lleida is La Suda, a fort taken from the Moors in 1149. The cathedral, founded in 1203, lies within the fort's walls, above the town. A lift descends from La Seu Vella to the Plaça de Sant Joan. The new cathedral is here, as is the reconstructed 13th-century town hall, the Paeria.

Poblet

See pp68–9.

Montblanc

Tarragona. Market: Tue, Fri. Festivals: Festa major (8–11 Sep). Museu Comarcal de la Conca de Barberà open Tue–Sun. Adm charge.

Medieval Montblanc is possibly Catalonia's finest piece of military architecture. At the Sant Jordi gate St George allegedly slew the dragon. The Museu Comarcal de la Conca de Barberà has displays on local crafts.

Santes Creus

Tarragona. Market: Sat, Sun. Festivals: Santa Llúcia (13 Dec). Monestir de Santes Creus open Tue–Sun except 25 Dec, 1 Jan. Adm charge.

The tiny village of Santes Creus is home to the prettiest of the "Cistercian triangle" monasteries. The other two, Vallbona de les Monges and Poblet, are nearby. The Monestir de Santes Creus was founded in 1150 by Ramon Berenguer IV during his reconquest of Catalonia. The Gothic cloisters have figurative sculptures, a style first permitted by Jaume II, who ruled from 1291 to 1327. His tomb is in the 12th-century church which features a rose window.

Vilafranca del Penedès

Barcelona. Market: Sat. Festivals: Fira de Mayo (2nd wk May), Festa major (end Aug). Museu del Vi open Tue–Sun. Adm charge.

This market town is set in the heart of Penedès, the main wine-producing region of Catalonia. The Museu del Vi (Wine Museum) documents the history of the area's wine trade. Local *bodegues* can be visited for wine tasting. Sant Sadurní d'Anoia, the capital of *cava*, Spain's sparkling wine, is 8 km (5 miles) to the north.

Monestir de Santes Creus, surrounded by poplar and hazel trees

Monestir de Poblet 🕒

The monastery of Santa Maria de
Poblet was the first and most important
of three sister monasteries, known as
the "Cistercian triangle". In 1835 it was
plundered and seriously damaged by
fire. Restoration began in 1930 and
monks returned in 1940.

The Abbey
*is in a valley
near the Riu
Francoli's
source.*

Dormitory

**The Gothic
Scriptorium**
*was converted
into a library
in the 17th
century.*

Museum

Wine cellar

**The 12th-
century Refectory**
*is a vaulted hall with
an octagonal fountain
and a pulpit.*

Museum

Royal doorway

The Cloisters *were built in the
12th and 13th centuries.*

VISITORS' CHECKLIST

Off N240, 10 km (6 mi) from
Montblanc. Open daily except
25–26 Dec, 1 Jan. Adm
charge. Services 8am daily;
10am, 1pm & 6pm Sun, public
hols.

The Chapterhouse
*is paved with the
tomb-stones of 11
abbots who died
between 1393
and 1693.*

Parlour
cloister

Sant Esteve
cloister

A Reredos
*behind the
stone altar
was carved in
alabaster by
Damià Forment
in 1527.*

New
sacristy

**The Abbey
Church** *has
three naves.*

Baroque
church
façade

The Royal Tombs *in
the pantheon of kings
were begun in 1359.*

Palm trees lining the waterfront at Sitges

Sitges 🅱

Barcelona. Market: Thu (summer). Festa major (22–27 Aug). Museu Cau Ferrat open Tue–Sun except public hols. Adm charge.

There are nine beaches at this seaside town. Lively bars and restaurants line its main boulevard, and there are examples of Modernista architecture amongst the '70s apartment blocks. Modernista artist Santiago Rusiñol bequeathed his collection of ceramics, sculptures, painting and ornate iron-work to the Museu Cau Ferrat. It is next to Sitges's landmark, the church of Sant Bartomeu i Santa Tecla.

Costa Daurada 🅲

Tarragona. Market: Tue, Thu. Museu Pau Casals open Tue–Sun. Free. Port Aventura open Mar–Jan. Adm charge.

The sandy beaches of the Costa Daurada (Golden Coast) run along the shores of Tarragona province. El Vendrell is an active port. The Museu Pau Casals in Sant Salvador (El Vendrell) is dedicated to the famous cellist. Port Aventura, to the south, is one of Europe's largest theme parks and has many attractions. Cambrils and Salou to the south are lively resorts – the others are low-key, family spots.

THE SARDANA

Catalonia's national dance (shown below in stone) is based on dancers forming a circle and counting complicated short- and long-step skips and jumps. Music is provided by an 11-person band. The sardana is performed during most festes and at special day-long gatherings called aplecs. In Barcelona it is danced on Saturday evenings in front of the cathedral and every Sunday evening at 6pm in the Plaça de Sant Jaume.

Tarragona ⑲

Tarragona. Market: Tue, Thu.
Festivals: Sant Magi (19 Aug),
Santa Tecla (23 Sep). Museu
Nacional Arqueològic de
Tarragona open Tue–Sun. Adm
charge. Museu de la Romanitat
open Tue–Sun. Adm charge.

Tarragona has many remnants of its Roman past. It was a base for the conquest of the peninsula by the Romans in the 3rd century BC. The avenue of Rambla Nova ends in sight of the ruins of the Amfiteatre Romà and the ruined church of Santa Maria del Miracle. Nearby is the Praetorium, a former Roman tower. It now houses the Museu de la Romanitat. This displays Roman and medieval finds, and has access to the excavated Roman circus, built in the 1st century AD. Next to the Praetorium is the Museu Nacional Arqueològic, with the most important Roman artifacts in Catalonia, including the pre-Roman stones on which the Roman wall is built. A 1-km (1,100-yd) archaeological walk stretches along the wall.

The remains of the Roman amphitheatre, Tarragona

Behind it is the 12th-century cathedral, built on the site of a Roman temple. The 13th-century cloister has Gothic vaulting, but the doorway is Romanesque. In the west of town is a 3rd- to 6th-century Christian cemetery.

Delta de L'Ebre ⑳

Tarragona. Eco-Museu open daily.
Adm charge.

Some 70 sq km (27 sq miles) of the Riu Ebre delta have been turned into a nature reserve, the Parc Natural del Delta de L'Ebre. In Deltebre there is an information centre and an Eco-Museu, with an aquarium containing species found in the delta. The area's main towns are Amposta and Sant Carles de la Ràpita – both good bases for exploring the reserve. The best places to see wildlife are along the shore, from the Punta del Fangar in the north to the Punta de la Banya in the south.

Tortosa ㉑

Tarragona. Market: Mon.
Festivals: Nostra Senyora de la
Cinta (1st wk Sep).

A ruined castle and medieval walls are clues to Tortosa's historical importance. The Moors held the city from the 8th century until 1148. The old Moorish castle, known as La Suda, is all that remains of their defences. The Moors also built a mosque in Tortosa in 914. Its foundations were used for the present cathedral, whose style is Gothic.

Getting Around

Barcelona is very compact and particularly well organized for visitors. Most areas are best visited on foot, an easy way to soak up the city's cultural and architectural riches. The metro is fast and easy to use, and the bus system covers the entire city.

Walking in Barcelona

Barcelona is so compact that it is a great place for walking, particularly the Old Town and Gràcia as well as the waterfront from Port Vell to Port Olímpic. The main tourist office in Plaça de Catalunya organizes guided walks, exploring the Roman and medieval history of the Barri Gòtic.

Cycling in Barcelona

Pedalling around the port, Barri Gòtic or Parc de la Ciutadella is a refreshing alternative to walking. Barcelona has over 70 km (43 miles) of bike lanes. The bike rental shop Un Cotxe Menys ("One Car Less") organizes group bike tours around the Old Town.

Driving in Barcelona

If you take your own car to Spain, a green card, a bail bond, vehicle registration, insurance documents, an EU or international driver's licence, passport, a country of origin sticker, spare light bulbs, first-aid kit, and a red warning triangle are required. Failure to comply will incur on-the-spot fines.

Parking

A pay-and-display system is in force from 9am to 2pm, 5pm to 8pm, Monday to Friday and all day Saturday. You can park in blue spaces for 1 to 2 euros per hour, or use an underground car park.

No parking sign

Travelling by Taxi

Taxis are yellow and black, display a green light when free, and most are metered, showing a minimum fee at the start of a journey. Increased rates apply after 10pm and at weekends.

One of Barcelona's taxis

Tickets and Travel Passes

A single fare on the metro, FGC, bus or nightbus costs €1.05. If you're in the city

Logo of the National ATESA car-rental company

Ticket machine for regionals, or regional trains (left) and rodalies, or local commuter trains (right).

for a few days, it's worth buying the T-10 ticket, valid for 10 trips on all three. Or get a two-, three-, four- or five-day pass that gives unlimited travel on public transport. Buy your tickets from the machines or attendants at all metro stations.

Metro

The five-line metro system is convenient, fast, easy to use and extensive. It is open from 5am (6am on Sundays) to midnight, and until 2am at weekends.

Using the FGC

The city's commuter rail system *Metro and FGC rail services sign* serves northern and eastern Barcelona, sharing several key stations with the metro, with the same prices and similar hours.

Buses

The bus system covers all of Barcelona. Bus stops are clearly marked and buses have their destinations on the front. For information on routes and schedules, call 010 or pick up a bus guide from tourist offices.

Nightbuses

There are about 15 *Nitbus* (nightbus) routes across the city, many of which pass through Plaça de Catalunya.

Barcelona bus stop

Bus Tours

The open-topped *Bus Turistic* is a grand way to experience the city's sights and sounds. The red route explores northern Barcelona, the blue route takes in the southern area. You can hop on and off as many times as you like.

Boat Tours

See the city from the sea on one of Les Golondrines' sightseeing boats. Trips last 35 minutes, departing every half-hour.

Cable Cars

Catch a cable car (*telefèric*) ride, for stunning views of the city. They depart from Montjuïc, Torre de Jaume I or Torre de Sant Sebastià.

TRAVEL INFORMATION

For general public transport information call **Barcelona Local Council**: 010. For intercity rail services (**RENFE**) information and credit card bookings tel: 902 24 02 02 (national); 902 24 34 02 (international). For **FGC** information tel: 93 205 15 15.

Survival Guide

Barcelona is relatively safe, but take care. Keep cards and money in a belt and avoid poorly lit areas at night. In a medical emergency, pharmacies can prescribe as well as advise. Report lost documents to your consulate and to the police.

MONEY

Euro bank notes

Currency

The euro (€) operates in Spain. Euro banknotes have seven denominations: 5, 10, 20, 50, 100, 200 and 500. Coin denominations are €2, €1, 50, 20 and 10 (silver or gold) and 5, 2 and 1 cents (bronze).

Banks

Generally, banks are open 8am–2pm on weekdays and some 4–8pm on Thursdays, 8am–2pm on Saturdays (except July to September). They tend to offer better exchange and commission rates.

Credit Cards

VISA and MasterCard are readily accepted in most places, American Express and Diner's Card less so. Obtain credit card cash advances from banks (or ATMs with a PIN number).

Changing Money

Avoid *bureaux de change* in tourist areas as commission rates are high and exchange rates poor. However, on the plus side, they stay open longer.

ATMs

Cash machines are the easiest way to access money without commission charges. Check that your PIN numbers work with foreign ATMs. Nearly all take VISA or MasterCard.

Traveller's Cheques

Buy traveller's cheques in Euros. All banks and larger stores cash them, as do any Banco Central Hispano or American Express (free of charge for their cheques) – and take your passport.

COMMUNICATIONS

Post Offices

The main post office at Pl Antoni López, open from 8.30am–9.30pm, Mon–Sat, 9am–2.30pm Sun, also offers fax and express mail services. Smaller offices are open 8.30am–8pm Mon–Fri and 10am–1pm Sat. Mailboxes are bright yellow. For letters and postcards, you can also buy stamps at an *estanc* (tobacconist).

Catalan mailbox

Telephones

Phone numbers begin with 93, and have seven subsequent digits. When calling overseas, dial 00 followed by the country code, area code and phone number.

Use a *Telefonica* phonecard or coins in public telephones (*cabines*). Buy cards from phone centres newsstands or, tobacconists.

Internet Cafés

Internet Cafés are dotted all over Barcelona, around Plaça de Catalunya and La Rambla particularly. Most are open until 11pm.

HEALTH AND SAFETY

Police

Victims of crime should contact local (*Guardia Urbana*) or national police (*Policia Nacional*). Petty crimes are rife, but more serious violence is rare.

Health Insurance

EU citizens can receive free medical care with a European Health Insurance Card, which you must obtain before travelling. Non-EU citizens should take out medical cover.

Hospitals

Three hospitals have 24-hour emergency rooms:
• Hospital de la Creu Roja de Barcelona:
Tel: 93 507 27 00
• Hospital de la Santa Creu de Sant Pau:
Tel: 93 291 90 00
• Hospital Clinic:
Tel: 93 227 54 00

Creu Roja

Red Cross ambulance sign

URGENCIES

Accident and Emergency sign

Doctors and Clinics

The tourist office can give information on English-speaking doctors. There are numerous walk-in clinics, including one near Plaça de Catalunya: Creu Blanca Open 9am–1pm, 4–7pm Mon–Fri, 9am–1pm Sat; Tel: 93 412 12 12

Dentists

Dental care is not covered by the EU health service. Dentists are usually on duty 9am–9pm weekdays at walk-in clinics, such as:
Clinica Dental Barcelona
Tel: 93 487 83 29

Front of a high-street farmàcia (pharmacy) in Catalonia

Pharmacies

Farmacies are marked by a large green cross, in neon. Pharmacists can offer advice in English at chemists near or on La Rambla, with many open 24 hours. Normal hours are 9am–2pm and 4.30–8pm. One pharmacy per neighbourhood stays open all night. Lists indicating this are on the pharmacy's front door.

EMERGENCY NUMBERS
All Emergency Nos
Tel: 112
Ambulance
Tel: 061
Police
Tel: 091 (national), 092 (local)

Index

Acknowledgments

Dorling Kindersley would like to thank the following people whose help and assistance contributed to the preparation of this book.

Design and Editorial
Publisher Douglas Amrine
Publishing Manager Vivien Antwi
Managing Art Editor Kate Poole
Cartography Casper Morris
Design Kavita Saha, Shahid Mahmood
Editorial Dora Whitaker
Production Controller Shane Higgins
Picture Research Ellen Root
DTP Jason Little
Jacket Design Simon Oon, Tessa Bindloss

Picture Credits

Every effort has been made to trace the copyright holders, and we apologize in advance for any omissions. We would be pleased to insert appropriate acknowledgments in any subsequent edition of this publication.

t = top; tl = top left; tc = top centre; tr = top right; cla = centre left above; ca = centre above; cra = centre right above; cl = centre left; c = centre; cr = centre right; clb = centre left below; cb = centre below; crb = centre right below; bl = bottom left; b = bottom; bc = bottom centre; br = bottom right.

The Publishers are grateful to the following individuals, companies and picture libraries for permission to reproduce their photographs:

ALAMY IMAGES: Andrew Bargeny 20b; Chad Ehlers 53t; Dalgleish Images 52bl; Neil Stechfield 23t; Oliver Bee 32cl; Richard Foot 52tl; Stephen Saks Photography 27t; CORBIS: Andrea Jemlo 38cl; Archivo Iconografico S.A. 33tl; Mark Stephenson 39cr; Owen Franken 9tl; Sandro Vannini 38br; NICK INMAN 52br; ©RED HEAD 12.

JACKET
Front – ALAMY IMAGES: G P Bowater front; DK IMAGES: Mike Dunning spine.

All other images © DORLING KINDERSLEY
For further information see www.DKimages.com.

Price Codes are for a three-course meal per person including tax, service and half a bottle of house wine
Cheap under €20
Moderate €20–€50
Expensive €50 or more

SPECIAL EDITIONS OF DK TRAVEL GUIDES

DK Travel Guides can be purchased in bulk quantities at discounted prices for use in promotions or as premiums. We are also able to offer special editions and personalized jackets, corporate imprints, and excerpts from all of our books, tailored specifically to meet your own needs.

To find out more, please contact:
(in the United States) **SpecialSales@dk.com**
(in the UK) **Sarah.Burgess@dk.com**
(in Canada) DK Special Sales at **general@tourmaline.ca**
(in Australia) **business.development@pearson.com.au**

Phrase Book

In Emergency

Help!	Auxili!	ow-**gzee**-lee
Stop!	Pareu!	**pah**-reh-oo
Call a doctor!	Telefoneu un metge!	teh-leh-fon-**ch**-oo oon **meh**-djuh
Call an ambulance!	Telefoneu una ambulància!	teh-leh-fon-**ch**-oo oo-nah ahm-boo-**lahn**-see-ah
Call the police!	Telefoneu la policia!	teh-leh-fon-**ch**-oo lah poh-lee-**see**-ah
Call the fire brigade!	Telefoneu els bombers!	teh-leh-fon-**ch**-oo uhlz boom-**behs**
Where is the nearest telephone?	On és el telèfon més proper?	on-ehs uhl tuh-leh-fon mehs proo-**peh**
Where is the nearest hospital?	On és l'hospital més proper?	on-ehs looss-pee-tahl mehs proo-**peh**

Communication Essentials

Yes	Sí	see
No	No	noh
Please	Si us plau	sees plah-oo
Thank you	Gràcies	**grah**-see-uhs
Excuse me	Perdoni	puhr-**thoh**-nee
Hello	Hola	**oh**-lah
Goodbye	Adéu	ah-they-**oo**

Useful Phrases

How are you?	Com està?	kom uhs-**tah**
Very well, thank you.	Molt bé, gràcies.	mol beh **grah**-see-uhs
Pleased to meet you.	Molt de gust.	mol duh **goost**
That's fine.	Està bé.	uhs-**tah** beh
Where is/are ...?	On és/són?	ohn ehs/sohn
How far is it to ...?	Quants metres/ kilòmetres hi ha d'aquí a ...?	kwahnz meh-truhs/kee-loh-muh-truhs yah dah-**kee** uh
Which way to ...?	Per on es va a ...?	puhr on uhs **bah** ah
Do you speak English?	Parla anglès?	par-lah an-**glehs**
I don't understand	No l'entenc.	noh luhn-teng
Could you speak more slowly, please?	Pot parlar més a poc a poc, si us plau?	pot par-**lah** mehs pok uh pok sees plah-oo

Useful Words

big	gran	gran
small	petit	puh-**teet**
hot	calent	kah-**len**
cold	fred	fred
open	obert	oo-**behr**
closed	tancat	tan-**kat**
left	esquerra	uhs-**kehr**-ruh
right	dreta	**dreh**-tuh
straight on	recte	**rehk**-tuh
entrance	entrada	uhn-**trah**-thuh
exit	sortida	**soor**-tee-thuh
toilet	lavabos/ serveis	luh-**vah**-boos sehr-**beh**-ees